SUB-MISSION

THE SILENT SERVICE

SUB-MISSION

THE SILENT SERVICE

Justin Teal

SUB-MISSION: THE SILENT SERVICE

Justin Teal

Copyright © 2023 by Justin Teal. All rights reserved.

This publication may not be reproduced, stored in an electronic system, or transmitted in any form or by any means, electronic, mechanical, photocopy, recording, or otherwise, without proper credit to the author. Brief quotations may be used without permission.

Some Scripture quotations are from the King James Version of the Bible. Some Scripture quotation are from The Amplified Bible. "Scripture quotations taken from the Amplified® Bible (AMP), Copyright © 2015 by The Lockman Foundation. Used by permission. lockman.org"

The author may be contacted at:

thedisciplesdialogue@gmail.com

Woodsong Publishing, Seymour, IN

Woodsongpublishing.com

Printed in the United States of America

ISBN 978-1-961482-05-0

CONTENTS

Foreword by Pastor McKillop

Foreword by Apostolic Review

Introduction

Chapter 1   BASIC TRAINING

Chapter 2   RECONNAISSANCE

Chapter 3   WHY NOT THE BEST

Chapter 4   ANTI-SUBMISSION

Chapter 5   CRUSH DEPTH

Chapter 6   SURFACING

Conclusion

FOREWORD

At the intersection of our human and spiritual existence lies an often misunderstood and underestimated concept—the biblical role of submission. It is a subject that has, for centuries, navigated through the currents of theological discourse, sometimes obscured by the fog of misinterpretation and misapplication. And, if misunderstood there, one can only imagine how this subject has been maligned in the arena of societal interpretation at large.

In a practical and thought-provoking manner, Justin Teal embarks on an insightful exploration of this concept, guided by the precision and clarity of a skilled submariner. Through the pages that follow, you will discover that submission is not a mark of weakness, nor is it a mandate for oppression. Rather, it is a divine call to return to proper spiritual alignment and harmony…both vertical and horizontal.

This book is not for the faint of heart. It enlists its reader to engage in the eternal conflict of conquering the self-damning, devious element of pride in your personal life. And yes, the one-word solution for overcoming the fatalistic effects of pride is submission. Everything within our fallen, human nature recoils at the very thought of submission. Satan understands this and attempts to capitalize on this reality. This has been the case since pride set up the original fall in the garden of Eden.

On this journey, you will discover that biblical submission, when lived out authentically, is not about losing one's identity but rather about finding it in a deeper way. In a world often dominated by the shallow pursuit of individualism and autonomy, profound liberty and victory is discovered when one embraces the depths of submission to a superior plan. In accordance with the pattern of the Lord's prayer, the submitted disciple prays: "THY Kingdom come. THY will be done…." It is not about me. It's about THEE, and THY WILL, Oh God.

This is witnessed in the account of Gideon leading his three hundred fearless warriors in a military conquest against the innumerable host of the Midianites. "And he said unto them, Look on me, and do likewise: and, behold, when I come to the outside of the camp, it shall be that, as I do, so shall ye do" (Judges 7:16-17). The instruction of Gideon to his followers was simple: Do as I do. Doesn't that sound a bit arrogant of Gideon? No. Not if you properly understand authority and submission.

When you are on the battlefield (or in the sea), there is no room for varying, prideful opinions. Commands are given to be followed. One maverick comrade breaking a pitcher and blowing a trumpet too soon would have thwarted the overall success of God's (and Gideon's) mission. It takes "sub mission" to the GREATER mission to achieve lasting victory. When this occurs, both personal and corporate victory is experienced. All of Israel benefited when the three hundred men submitted to Gideon's military directives.

So, dear reader, prepare to submerge yourself into the exploration of submission. Justin Teal has provided us with the tools and insights to navigate these dark waters, and as we journey together, may we emerge with a newfound understanding (and appreciation) of the biblical role of submission and a deeper connection to the divine purpose that beckons us from the deep. Bon voyage!

Pastor McKillop

FOREWORD

There are certain books that leave a lasting mark on one's spiritual journey. Often, it's not the ones that top the bestseller charts but the concise, thought-provoking works that transform our hearts. My personal library contains numerous brief but impactful books that have reshaped my outlook on life, church, and God. In this regard, Justin Teal's Sub-Mission is a prime example of a short but meaningful book. As I read through Teal's book, it transported me back to the early years in the ministry, a period during which I wrestled with numerous misconceptions about leadership in the church. They were years which required patient correction and a willingness to submit to godly authority. Unquestionably, submission, and the readiness to serve the Lord, even in roles that frequently go unnoticed and underappreciated, constitute the fundamental key to effective leadership. Indeed, as Teal emphasizes "it is…very rewarding to know that your life of silent service is ultimately what enables those above sea level to enjoy their freedom."

In my early stages of my spiritual life, leadership books like Shoe Leather Commitment by J. Oswald Sanders and the Spiritual Man by Watchman Nee left an indelible mark in my thinking. These books cultivated an understanding of the type of commitment that is required to serve the Lord and leave a lasting impact within His kingdom. It seems to me that Sub-Mission represents this same type of book. It will compel those who read it to confront a critical truth: that often, our struggles with authority do not stem from authority itself but are rooted in inward pride. It is pride that must first be dealt with if we ever expect to grow into the holy leaders that God has called us to be.

Teal leverages his personal background as a submariner to construct a framework for the concept of spiritual submission. In this context, he underscores the importance of teamwork, respect, and trust in authority as critical factors for the successful execution of the mission. The submarine, unlike other vessels, fulfills its mission by operating in the unseen, "beneath the waters." This distinctive characteristic becomes a powerful analogy for illustrating the spiritual dynamics that occur between the "XO," (the pastor) and the crew (the church). Teal reminds us that the cornerstone of effective leadership, and for that matter effective followership, is bound within the concept of submission.

Sub-Mission serves as a succinct yet valuable introduction to the topic of spiritual leadership. Its straightforward but persuasive principles will aid those who are pursuing any sort of ministry among God's people. This small book has reminded me that no matter what our position in God's kingdom, there is no room for pride; we are called to display a Christ-like submission to our Lord, our pastors, our ministry leaders, and one another. Teal has again convinced me that within the Church, no role is insignificant – all saints are called to be servants of the Lord, and at the heart of this sacred service resides the essential quality of being "submitted."

Apostolic Review

INTRODUCTION

I can see the irony in writing a book detailing the battle against pride in my life. So, at the outset, let me make it very clear, I do not claim to have yet, fully rid myself of this spirit-killing, flesh-fulfilling condition. My intention in writing this book is not to give you a simple five-step program that ensures you a life free of the tendencies that lead to pride. However, my intention is for you to become keenly aware of the early indicators that pride may well be infiltrating your heart: that you may be able to launch a preemptive strike to avoid the casualty that is your own soul.

I understand that I am not victorious until I have finished my race and I hear those precious words, "...*Well done, thou good and faithful servant: thou hast been faithful over a few things, I will make thee ruler over many things: enter thou into the joy of thy Lord*" *(Matthew 25:21 KJV)*.

While I am not an advocate of war, I understand that humans have, from the beginning, been at odds with one another and will continue to do so until the return of our Lord and Savior, Jesus Christ. But rather than just being at odds with one another, we too often overlook the battle within ourselves: the war against one's own fleshly and deceitful ways. The enemy inside of each of us that I am referring to is most well known as **PRIDE**. This book will outline my personal history with this unforgiving trait and how—through the help of the Holy Spirit, Biblical principles, and Godly council—I am able to daily win the battle within myself, for myself. Having not yet won the war, I fight the good fight daily, and with God's help, you too, will be able to overcome the enemy that is too much of you.

I know you are probably a good person. You probably pray a lot and pay your tithes. You may be the first one at church when the doors are open and the last one to leave. You may even be a Sunday school teacher, youth leader, or even a pastor. But one thing is certain: you are not exempt from facing this silent killer: pride. As a matter of fact, if you find yourself defensive at my indication that you too may be dealing with some pride of your own, you may have more pride than you realize. There is nothing more dangerous than an unknown enemy lurking in your territory, watching your every move, studying you, just waiting on you to let down your guard so they can attack.

If you haven't yet caught on, I liken the idea of battling with pride to that of modern-day warfare. After all, we are in a war, a war against the flesh. Make no mistake, I understand that the Word of God plainly teaches us, *"For we wrestle not against flesh and blood, but against principalities, against powers, against the rulers of the darkness of this world, against spiritual wickedness in high places." (Ephesians 6:12 KJV)*

So, how do you defeat the enemy if the enemy

is within you, without destroying yourself in the process? How do you identify such a threat while constantly talking yourself out of it, chalking it up to the fact that you are simply misunderstood by others and that you aren't really the problem; instead, they are. Often, the hardest enemy to identify and defeat is the one unseen. Camouflaged neath the guise of godly humility, pride can and will attack. Pride is often a silent killer, a marksman who rarely misses its target, a veteran assassin.

It is with this acknowledgment that I deploy you, a soldier in the army of the Lord, to engage in this battle, knowing that if you can learn **submission**, you will be victorious. I can almost see the look of confusion upon your face. What does submission have to do with defeating pride in my life? In my experience, having learned the hard way, when you finally learn submission, you are well on your way to completely eradicating yourself from this wretched spirit of pride. Again, that is not to say that I no longer deal with pride and have fully mastered the art of submission, having written a book about it. As a matter of fact, the more I learn to submit, the more I see the need in my own personal life.

So, let us now take a deep dive (pun intended) into the unfamiliar territory of submission, that we may be able to once and for all defeat our formidable foe, pride. To better help us understand the content of this book, let us tap into our child-like imaginations. Imagine with me, you have just enlisted in the Navy and our country is amid a war with an unidentified enemy. You are a smart person, so you understand that this is not going to be easy, and many will lose their lives in the process, but for the sake of your freedom and the freedom of your loved ones, you proceed: you enlist.

Now that we have enlisted, we are ready to board our new home, a state of the art, ballistic missile, nuclear submarine. Here we go…

> *"The reason why many are still troubled, still seeking, still making little forward progress is because they haven't yet come to the end of themselves. We're still trying to give orders and interfering with God's work within us."*
>
> *— A. W. Tozer*

1
BASIC TRAINING

As we begin our mission, boarding the submarine that is representative of a submitted life, we have a moment, a reality check. We have simulated this before in basic training. We have trained for hundreds of hours, prepared for worst case scenarios but nothing could have adequately prepared us for real life in this arena. No amount of training or advanced simulation could ready us for the real thing; that is not to say that training is unvaluable. As a matter of fact, without proper training, you are sure to fail.

The US Navy Recruit Training Command (RTC) lasts eight to ten weeks. Afterward, recruits receive advanced skills at Navy A School where some will spend up to two additional years preparing for their first deployment. Make no mistake, while you may or may not agree with our government's political policies and procedures, it is in their best interest, as well as yours, to adequately train young men and women before sending them into battle. The government benefits from the protection of our military personnel, so the United States is not afraid to spend money on training ($344 Billion in 2022).

That said, let me connect our story to our spiritual reality. You and I have enlisted into the Lords military, and you are a great asset to Him and to His kingdom. You provide a great service to our King, and He has invested so much in you to ensure your success. When you made the decision to believe in Him, turn away from your sin, and begin to live for God, you joined a team: the winning team. Some would say that this is when God first began to train and equip you, but I disagree; it was much earlier in your life. Much like the governments of this world that invest in advertising to gain the attention of young patriots, our God has been trying to capture your attention your whole life. And just like the United States heavily used the image of Uncle Sam with his finger pointed eagerly at the citizens of the United States during World War I, stating, "I WANT YOU," our God wants you!

Unlike the governments of this world, Jesus doesn't simply desire you so that you may fight for His protection. Frankly, He does not need our protection. It is we that need Him. God desires you because of His love toward you. A love that is incomparable, unexplainable, and downright unfathomable. He doesn't need you, yet He wants you. He could have done things differently, but He chose you. The investment that God has made in you is reason enough for you to gladly join Him in the fight against the spiritual wickedness of this world.

Sometimes the greatest outcome is the result of an unrelenting effort. There are endless

SUB-MISSION: The Silent Service

applications here, but I will choose the following:

- The Wright Brothers, after many failed attempts, successfully invented the world's first motor-operated airplane, ultimately leading to the sound barrier being broken by an aircraft that was pushed to the point of shaking and coming apart, before success.

- The first deployable US submarine in 1775, named *Turtle*, was unsuccessful in all its attempts to affix explosives to the undersides of British warships during the American Revolutionary War. While unsuccessful in its time, it ultimately paved the way for the very capable submarines of today.

We need training. None of us are born with the know-how or experience that we will need to be victorious in the battle against pride. In fact, pride would have us convinced that we are not in need of training, and we can figure everything out on our own. The fact remains, Satan is a liar. He has long been a liar and he will always be a liar. The Word of God teaches us that there is no truth in him. We need training. Be it Godly council from our pastor, Apostolic mentoring, seminars, YouTube videos, cassette tapes, podcasts, books etc., we need to consume as much knowledge and wisdom as we can from anywhere we can, given that the information is doctrinally sound.

Just as a firefighter doesn't wait until they

are standing before a structure fire, and a police officer doesn't wait until the bank robbery is under way to begin training for these scenarios, we should not delay in training for the great things of God's kingdom. No, we may not fully understand what God has planned for our lives at a young age (if you will be a pastor, teacher, evangelist etc.), but we can train in areas that will assist us no matter the calling that awaits us in our future. Whether we are to be used in any of the five-fold ministry (apostles, prophets, evangelists, pastors, teachers), we should begin early in our lives to seek out Godly wisdom. After all, we are training for a battle. Remember? We are not joining the Boy Scouts of America or some other futile club. By studying the things of God from a young age, we will be more prepared than most when the day of battle begins, and it will begin.

At the time of this writing, my children are ages 10 and 8. I thank God that I can say, my children were born into the church and are now 2nd generation Apostolics. They have been raised in the fear of God and taught from birth to put God first in everything they do. My son (10) was filled with the Holy Ghost at the age of 7 during Family Camp at the Virginia District campground in 2020. My daughter (8) was recently filled with the Holy Ghost (2023) while in our weekly Bible study in a neighboring city. I took to heart when the Scripture said, *"Train up a child in the way he should go: And when he is old, he will not depart from it"(Proverbs 22:6 KJV).*

SUB-MISSION: THE SILENT SERVICE

I delight in knowing that my children will not depart from the faith, having raised them in "the way" (Jesus is the way). But nobody, including my children, will make it to Heaven by accident. If we are to enter the Kingdom of God for eternity, it will be because we were trained.

Maybe you are not a youth anymore. However, you are not exempt from the training phase. You may be like me, coming into the church later in life, but thank God, He has the same reward (Heaven) for those who have been in the church their whole lives and those who are born again later in life. While a child receives their training by listening and obeying, it's not that different for us adults. We tend to over-complicate things, but the truth of the matter is, it's as simple as listening and obeying. Of course, there is a deeper depth that we will get into, but a good place to start is listening and obeying.

The disciples did not start out knowing how to build Jesus' Kingdom. As a matter of fact, they hardly knew how to pray. We know this because they asked Jesus how to pray. *"And it came to pass, that, as he was praying in a certain place, when he ceased, one of his disciples said unto him, Lord, teach us to pray, as John also taught his disciples"(Luke 11:1 KJV).*

Even when you have been around long enough to learn a few things, you cannot afford to become over-ambitious, letting pride creep in the back door, because it will. I have been in ministry for over a decade, and I am more aware now than ever before of my need to be trained. It's not because I have not applied myself and am still at the same spiritual place I was when I began. No, I have grown. I have taught kids' classes, adult Sunday School, prison ministry, been the Men's Ministry Director, been on the worship team, and am also on the church board. Though I have held several positions within the church, I am still in need of training. I look to my pastor as my spiritual leader who knows that he can correct me without it causing me to get mad and quit. Why? Because I am being trained. Every moment of every day, I need to be learning. And let me be clear, this is no small task, to be able to be corrected without it causing bitterness and the desire to quit. The one thing that enables me to not be offended, but rather be corrected, is **submission**.

David was submitted, not only to God but to his spiritual leader, Saul. Even when David knew that Saul was in the wrong, he respected God enough to respect God's chosen leader. You may be asked to do the same, to concede to your spiritual leader even when you think or know that you are in the right. You know, it's not about being right. That is an issue that arises out of pride itself.

I have realized I don't have to be right, but I must be submitted. Not that I want anyone facing the judgement of God, but if my spiritual leader gets something wrong, that is between him and God. It has no bearing on me if I am doing what God asked me to do. Make no mistake, I am not suggesting we follow incorrect doctrine or submit ourselves to someone just because of their title. I am, however, suggesting that we remain submitted to our leaders

SUB-MISSION: The Silent Service

if they are submitted to God, even if they make a mistake along the way. After all, they are human, just as you and I are. We would do well to follow Jesus' example and rather than ridiculing, we should pray for them. We should protect them.

I suppose that it would be misleading of me if I were to avoid making it clear that I get it wrong lots of times. There are times when I must check myself, look in the mirror and say, "You need to pray." A recent example (after beginning this book on submission): It was a Sunday morning like any other. My wife, kids, and I got up and got ready for church. I was excited. I was having a good morning and had an expectation in my spirit about what God would do that morning. We arrived at church early, greeted a few folks, and even had a good time of prayer before service began. Church began as the worship team led us into the wonderful presence of God, and I got involved. I was up front worshiping, jumping, and singing at the top of my lungs. I could feel the Spirit of God moving in the atmosphere. We had adult Sunday school, announcements, and corporate prayer, and everything was fine. It was then time for pastor to deliver the Word of God, and I was primed and ready. He began preaching, and it wasn't long before the smile fell from my face, the excitement went away, and I was being offended by most of what was being preached.

How in the world could I have gone from being so in tune with what was happening all morning, to being offended and quickly shutting down? Was the pastor really being offensive? Was he in the wrong? I sat there bitterly and watched as most of the church was often standing to their feet, clapping their hands in agreeance with what God was speaking though our pastor. "Amen," they shouted as I sat in disbelief. I can't believe they are not as offended as I am, I thought. Well, the message ended, and the altar call was given. I wasn't so mad that I wouldn't pray, so down to my knees I went. I buried my face in the chair and began to repeat these words, "God, if I am wrong, reveal it to me." In my mind, I was accusing my pastor of being blatantly offensive, but I didn't speak a word of it to anyone until I got home. My wife knows me better than anyone else, and so she knew that I was upset about something. She finally pried it out of me, and when it came loose, it got messy. I unloaded to her about how offended I was. She kept her cool and tried to speak some sense into me and told me that she didn't feel that way at all. I vowed to go back and watch the service that was uploaded to Facebook to prove that what I had felt was true.

Well, the next morning, one of the first things on my mind was how foolish I felt for acting that way. I remember the Lord quickening in my spirit, "Aren't you writing a book on submission and here you are, so easily offended and quick to take matters into your own hands?" I was smitten. I believe that this was a lesson from God, making sure that I was able to stand where I would soon be trying to help others. Thank God, I did not let that stop me nor will I allow a misstep on my part to keep me from teaching others, so they may learn from my experiences and not make the same mistakes.

SUB-MISSION: The Silent Service

Don't be afraid to be wrong. Don't be afraid to face the familiar feeling of disappointment when you make a mistake. Don't be so proud that you are unwilling to look in the mirror and say to yourself, "Suck it up and go pray." Can you imagine how David Bushnell (inventor of the *Turtle* – submarine 1775) felt when his invention that was sure to help Washington win the American Revolutionary War, failed on all fronts? I cannot imagine that he was very proud of himself. In his own mind, he may have even felt like a fool: much like I felt after my recent heap of ignorance. But even after his many failures, his leader, General Washington, wrote a letter to Thomas Jefferson regarding David Bushnell and his failed invention that said:

> *"Bushnell came to me in 1776 recommended by Governor Trumbull and other respectable characters… Although I wanted faith myself, I furnished him with money, and other aids to carry it into execution. He labored for some time ineffectually and, though the advocates for his scheme continued sanguine, he never did succeed. One accident or another was always intervening. I then thought, and still think, that it was an effort of genius; but that a combination of too many things were requisite…"*
>
> *Turtle [Submarine]* – Wikipedia

Sometimes when we fail, we are too close to see the good that remains. Often, it takes an outsider, in our case, Jesus, to see the good that remains inside each of us. Remember, you are not yet a veteran. You may be in basic training (a new convert), or you may be an officer within your ranks (one of the fivefold ministries), but one thing is certain, if you are reading this book, you have not yet won the battle. The battle wages on as you continue to war against the enemy of your soul and your flesh (pride). Remember, not if, but when you mess up the next time, 'I am in training.' We cannot afford to quit now because our friends, co-workers, and family are counting on us to keep fighting.

In the US Navy Seal training, there is a brass bell that hangs in the middle of the compound for all the students to see. All you must do to quit is ring the bell. Ring the bell and you no longer must wake up at 5:00 AM. Ring the bell and you no longer must take freezing cold swims. Ring the bell and you no longer must run, do the obstacle course, the PT, and you no longer must endure the hardships of training. All you must do is ring the bell to get out. If you want to change the world, don't ever, ever ring the bell.

Basic training is hardly "basic," as if it were common knowledge, understood easily by the swath of novice submariners; contrariwise, basic training is hard. It is foundational, irreplaceable, paramount knowledge that ultimately is the difference between wars won or lost. It requires a complex plethora of information not only to be heard, but understood, and not only understood, but obeyed to the nth degree.

One who stops learning (training) begins dying. The most expert in any arena trains constantly and consistently. The gold medal is most often given to the individual who has trained the most, played the least, and is rewarded as such. A good friend of mine once said, "I would do ANYTHING to be able to play the piano...," to which his wife wittingly replied, "ANYTHING but practice." How true of most of us, not to put you in a category you don't belong in, but most of us are the same way. We would love to do something, be something, but we are not willing to put in the work or in our case, the training to accomplish said goal. If you want to be the best at something, you need to train as if your life depends on it. For submariners, their lives, as well as the lives of 300,000,000 plus other Americans, do in fact depend on their basic training.

*"Unheard they work, unseen they win.
That is the custom of "The Trade."*

—*Rudyard Kipling—The Trade*

2
RECONNAISSANCE

Reconnaissance, better known by its abbreviated name, recon, may be an unfamiliar word to you unless you have spent time in the military or have played much Call of Duty. Reconnaissance simply means, the exploration of an area by military forces to obtain information about enemy forces, terrain, and other activities. Now that we are submariners in the Navy and have been adequately trained, our first mission is recon. The XO (executive officer) has given the order for you and me to investigate a potential threat that has appeared on our sonar screen.

Here is a good place to insert the fact that our modern-day warships and submarines are equipped with the world's most advanced technology. The United States of America is in a class of the elite when it comes to military capability. We are commonly placed among two other key players of military might in what some call, The Big Three (US, China, and Russia). Laying aside the desire to debate who leads this nuclear trilemma, none of them are ill equipped when it comes to technical advances.

Back to our story... We intently inspect the activity on our active sonar screen, careful to take note of any sign of danger lurking in the dark distance. Some would be so naïve as to think that the submariner who watches the sonar screen is somehow less important than the submariner responsible for activating the nuclear weaponry on board: not so. Each submariner on board plays a significant role in the success of the ship and the mission at large. The sonar room cannot say, I have no need of the nuclear weapons room, and the nuclear weapons room cannot say, I have no need of the chef in the kitchen. There is Scripture for that too:

> *And the eye cannot say unto the hand, I have no need of thee: nor again the head to the feet, I have no need of you. Nay, much more those members of the body, which seem to be more feeble, are necessary:*
>
> *1 Corinthians 12:21-22 KJV*

Recon is not always the most exciting job, but it is equally important. You see, knowing or not knowing something in the Navy may be the difference between life and death. Stealth is key in everything we do down here. When you become a submariner, you understand that you are signing up for near silence and invisibility for up to three months at a time. The only time you will be able to

SUB-MISSION: The Silent Service

connect to the internet long enough to send an email is when the sub surfaces. But remember, every time you send out a signal, you are letting everyone know your exact location. You lose your ability to remain unseen.

When we embark on a sub mission, we need to be prepared to disappear for a while. The best Navy submarine is the one that is untraceable, out of sight, and out of mind. This is how we retain our upper hand in all situations. It's not about who is the loudest, most intimidating, or who is seen the most. No, there is power in being below, lowering yourself into the depths of a quiet place, watching and listening. If you don't know we are here and we know you are there, we have done our jobs correctly.

The sonar is picking up a faint signal. It could be something, or it could be nothing. But one thing is certain: we are not going to stand idly by and not investigate. One of the biggest mistakes we can make is to ignore a potential threat. We've heard of the snowball effect, right? It starts out small but as it rolls down the hill, it gains momentum and mass, getting bigger and bigger until it is out of control. We cannot take that chance here. Could it be a whale, an offshore fishermen's boat? Of course. But it just as easily could be an unhappy enemy sub who has us in their sights, ready to take us out. Inaction is dangerous.

Let's take a break from the story and deal with this issue. If you simply attempt to ignore the issue of pride, hoping that it will just go away, you are sadly mistaken. Also, you were trained better than to think that. Pride, if unchecked, will destroy you before you are fully aware of the damage that has been done. Pride is as dangerous as any nuclear submarine: even more so to our soul. Do not take for granted that you said a five-minute prayer this morning and the devil will leave you alone. A five-minute prayer life will not keep your flesh in subjection, let alone, the devil at bay.

    I have dealt with pride my whole life. Sometimes it came in the form of me thinking that I was better than other people, but most of the time it was simply not believing that God could help someone like me. Both stem from a spirit of pride. Thankfully, I grew up in a home where we struggled financially more than we thrived. I know that may seem like an odd statement to make, but I believe that not having the nicest things growing up kept me humble a lot of the time. I couldn't make fun of kids wearing Starter brand (Walmart) clothes, because I was one of them. I couldn't bash others for living in a small house, because we had a small house. There was no room for me to taunt others about their moms' 1977 Chevy Impala (beater) that you had to start with a flathead screwdriver, because that is what we had.

    Sadly, most swords have two edges, and if one side doesn't get you, the other side probably will. As blessed as I was not to be raised to be some uppity rich kid who looked down on those who had less, I believe this is what shaped me into the man I was to become when I finished school and got out into the real world. When I realized that I could work and have nice things and I could make something out of myself, I hit the ground running. Everything became personal to me. I became very ambitious, probably overly ambitious about everything. I thought, 'I can do it, I can handle it, I am strong enough,' etc. Well, it turns out that I cannot do it all, I cannot handle everything, and I am not nearly strong enough. I was in a pickle. I didn't want to live life broke and scraping the bottom of the proverbial barrel, and at the same time I was creating a monster that I couldn't afford to keep feeding.

Even to this day I am kind of ambitious. Just ask my wife who has put up with me for almost twelve years now. I exhaust her with my constant desire to do more and become more and better myself. But this way of life is not without its own problems. It is a breeding ground for pride as I would soon find out. Pride almost ruined me. Pride almost ruined my marriage, my relationship with God, and my eternity. Pride is so dangerous, and from what I would come to learn, the antidote for pride is submission. So, let's get back to our story because the unidentified object's signal in the sonar room is getting stronger, and our concern is growing.

Our fellow submariners who are responsible for all things involving sonar have confirmed that the signal is indeed an enemy submarine. There is currently no sign of hostile activity, and the chances are they do not even know that we are here. We have done our due diligence in remaining silent, not sending or receiving any messages that would give up our position. But when you are this close to the enemy, everything is on the line. One wrong move and you could go from having the advantage of being unseen to being a target.

The XO has given the order, "Hold your position." In other words, do not make a move, be still, remain silent, and await further instruction. Everyone is on edge as tensions above the surface are giving way to instructions that the chief of the boat is receiving below. Here and now, communication is the key to success. Any individual aboard our sub who does not follow the instructions of the XO to the letter would put the lives of everyone else at risk.

I believe that is part of the problem that comes along with pride; when you are consumed with yourself, you aren't thinking about the lives of others. But when you realize that every decision you make effects more than just yourself, you just may reconsider your actions. War does not only affect the XO, the submariners aboard, or even their families. War reaches far and wide, affecting the lives of many thousands and even millions around the world. It is at this moment that you and I remember the importance of being submitted. The XO gives the instruction, and we don't argue, no matter our opinion.

If I have not made it obvious yet, the XO in our story represents the spiritual leader in our life, our pastor. I hope you have a pastor. If you do not currently, you need to make this a priority. Not because we cannot have a relationship with God without a pastor, but we would never understand the nature of God without first understanding the hierarchy of His Kingdom. You see, God in our story is the unseen authority, the Commander in Chief. It is Him Who has the ultimate say as to what happens because He owns the boat. Also, He owns the water that the boat is in. He owns it all, and without Him, there would be nothing.

God is aware of every moving part, and while we are unaware, His instruction is, "Trust me, for I know how to protect you and bring you the victory." Often time, the XO (pastor) is the direct mediator between the Commander in Chief (God) and the submariners (church). God provides instruction, guidance, wisdom, etc. to the pastor to enable the pastor to operate in that same authoritative instruction: the Word of God. Make no mistake, we are immediately in submission to our XO but ultimately to the Commander in Chief. You cannot be submitted to one and not the other, because they operate under the same authority.

You see, the XO is only as good an XO as he is submitted to the ultimate authority. Another way to say this is, you are not the only one who must be in submission. Everyone is subject to the rule and reign of the unseen authority: God. Aboard this submarine we must trust that the instructions and orders that we receive from our XO are not just his opinion but are ultimately coming from the top down. At the very least, if the XO was not given direct input in an urgent matter, to keep our position unknown and the crew safe, we must have faith that the XO is operating with the understanding of the

Commander in Chief's desires. Trust your XO, trust your pastor.

> *Obey them that have the rule over you, and submit yourselves: for they watch for your souls, as they that must give account, that they may do it with joy, and not with grief: for that is unprofitable for you.*
>
> *Hebrews 13:17 KJV*

Submission is not laying down, rolling over, and becoming a 'yes man,' shallow as that would be. No, the depths of submission are far deeper, even more so than the Mariana Trench which is at least 10,984 meters, or roughly 6.825 miles deep. One does not stumble upon a life of submission, just as one does not accidentally become a Navy submariner. Submission is steeped in intentionality, driven by purpose and a desire to become one of the few who truly understand the true meaning of 'The Silent Service.' Submission, like love, is not proud or loud. It does not boast and does not need recognition. One who is submitted is completely content in keeping their silence, obeying the instruction given, and awaiting their opportunity to glory in exuberant shouts of victory after the war is over.

Love endures with patience and serenity,

SUB-MISSION: THE SILENT SERVICE

love is kind and thoughtful, and is not jealous or envious; love does not brag and is not proud or arrogant. It is not rude; it is not self-seeking; it is not provoked [nor overly sensitive and easily angered]; it does not take into account a wrong endured. It does not rejoice at injustice, but rejoices with the truth [when right and truth prevail]. Love bears all things [regardless of what comes], believes all things [looking for the best in each one], hopes all things [remaining steadfast during difficult times], endures all things [without weakening].

1 Corinthians 13:4-7 AMP

Back in the sonar room, the XO has given the all-clear. The enemy sub passed and was unaware of our presence; we had done our jobs correctly. The crew is instructed to proceed with normal operations and there is a sigh of relief from the crew. You and I, newly enlisted submariners, find we are surrounded with people from all walks of life. Some are just as inexperienced as us, and some are veteran submariners. It's nice to know that we are not alone. As a matter of fact, had each one of these individuals not answered the call to serve alongside us, we would surely have been doomed to failure.

If our basic training taught us one thing, it was, we need one another. Brothers and sisters, we are united together, bound not only by the confines of a steel capsule but bound together in our lives' calling, to serve and protect our homeland: to fight for the freedom of those unable to fight. There is comfort in knowing that the captain of the boat has been in this situation before. It calms our nerves knowing that the lieutenant is a veteran sailor, with only victories under his belt. Nothing is needed more than the words of inspiration from our peers as we hold our breath, unable to blink as we watch an enemy nuclear sub pass through our territory.

  Recon is all about learning. The more you know, the more you see, the more you learn. It is amazing to watch the XO at work during a reconnaissance mission. His life experience, position, and direct communication with the unseen authority arrests the attention of all those in his presence. When he speaks, it is with authority and clarity. There is no trace of question in the tone of his voice. When he gives the command, whatever it may be, there is an assurance that rests upon the crew, knowing that our best interest lies in his every decision.

  You should never embark on a mission without complete confidence that you will learn something along the way. To plunge the depths of submission without the attitude of a student, eager to learn something while deployed, is a sure sign that you will likely fail. Submission is a mindset, an attitude that seeks no self-preservation. Submission is a selfless relinquishing of control to learn a skillset that will benefit the world at large.

SUB-MISSION: The Silent Service

You may have never been on a sub mission before. This may be your first attempt at this kind of life. While it's wildly different from the comfort of 'normal' life, it is also very rewarding to know that your life of silent service is ultimately what enables those above sea level to enjoy their freedoms. You have surely heard the adage, "freedom isn't free." No one can understand that better than one who has given their life to serve aboard a nuclear armed submarine for months at a time for the sake of others. There is a cost to knowledge. How much you learn greatly depends on how much you are willing to pay. How much recon are you willing to do?

Of course, our personal survival is paramount. For we are surely unable to help another if we are dead. Every submariner aboard this sub must first protect themselves before they can become of service to others. We too, must work out our own salvation as the Scripture states, to ensure that we can then go on to pull others out of the fire that they may find themselves in.

> *Wherefore, my beloved, as ye have always obeyed, not as in my presence only, but now much more in my absence, work out your own salvation with fear and trembling.*
>
> *Philippians 2:12 KJV*

And others save with fear, pulling them out of the fire; hating even the garment spotted by the flesh.

Jude 1:23 KJV

As you endeavor to submit yourself to the XO and ultimately to the Commander in Chief, you must understand that your first mission is to learn. If you cannot walk away from a mission and say, I learned a lesson there, you were not properly submitted. It's likely that those who fail to learn anything from their time of so-called submission, spent their time trying to teach rather than trying to learn. Everyone wants to be the boss until it's time to make the boss's decisions. Let us lay aside our prideful ambitions and submit ourselves to our spiritual leadership that we may be an asset rather than a liability.

3
WHY NOT THE BEST

In 1952, a young Naval Academy graduate had the opportunity to sit across from the father of America's nuclear Navy, Admiral Hyman Rickover, for an interview. It was the custom of Admiral Rickover to personally interview every single candidate for the submarine service. These interviews are said to have lasted hours as Admiral Rickover questioned each graduate on a plethora of topics such as tactics, physics, history, strategy, and literature.

During this specific interview, the young graduate was asked, "Where were you ranked in your class at the Naval Academy?" Relieved at the question, the graduate gladly responded, "I was ranked 59th in a class of 840, sir." The graduate was sure to receive some high praise or at the very least, a nod of approval; rather, he received a stint of silence followed by another question: "Did you always do your best?"

The graduate opened his mouth with the intention of uttering a resounding, "Yes sir," but he quickly remembered times when, at the Academy, he could have learned more about their allies, enemies, weapons, and strategy. Unwilling to lie to his superior, who likely already knew of his imperfections, the young graduate gulped and said, "No sir, I didn't always do my best." The intimidating Admiral quietly peered across the desk for what seemed to be an eternity before turning his chair, ending the interview, but not before asking one final question, which the young graduate would not soon forget. Admiral Rickover asked, "Why not?" To that, the shaken interviewee stood and quietly walked out of the room as he knew that his answer would prove to be inadequate, leaving him unfit for the silent service.

Shame has the tendency to silence us in the face of accountability. Sure, this young graduate could have pleaded his case, making excuses like we often do. But talking in circles, beating around the bush, and playing the blame game never amounts to much. The Scripture is correct when it says: *"But if ye will not do so, behold, ye have sinned against the LORD: and be sure your sin will find you out" (Numbers 32:23 KJV).*

Sin, or in the case of this aspiring Navy graduate, the lack of his best, had found him out. Make no mistake, the results of a lack of our best may not immediately show up, but sooner or later, what has been done in secret will be visible to all. *"For nothing is secret, that shall not be made manifest; neither any thing hid, that shall not be known and come abroad" (Luke 8:17 KJV).*

Thankfully, all is not lost when your less than perfect past shows up, most often in less-than-ideal

SUB-MISSION: THE SILENT SERVICE

circumstances. As a friend of mine once said, "There is a method to madness." God will never allow something to harm or destroy you. However, He will allow you to go through the fire as He did with Hananiah, Mishael, and Azariah, more commonly known as Shadrach, Meshach, and Abednego. But be of good cheer, for He will not let you go through the fire alone; He will be there with you. The fire is not meant to destroy you. It is meant to teach you (or someone else) something. It is meant to bring out the best in you.

I once told my son that everyone makes mistakes. It's okay to make mistakes. Just make sure that you learn from your mistakes. As my pastor once told me, "The sin is not in falling. The sin is in staying down." Allow these gentle reminders to wash over your mind as you remember all the many failures of your past. Remember, you may not have always done your best but that doesn't have to be the case today. Today, you can choose to give your best.

Considering Admiral Rickover's stern but commendable interview techniques, former US President, Jimmy Carter, entitled his book, *Why Not the Best*, which served as a tool to create transparency between the US government and the people. *Why Not the Best* later became the theme of his presidential campaign. It is a legitimate question to be asked, whether by one of our peers or even by ourselves.

No matter the circumstances, we should endeavor to do our best. But why? Why is it important to do our best? What are the consequences to those who are determined to do less than their best? Isn't 80% effort better than 0%? Well, let us investigate the topic at hand to answer the pointed question, why not the best?

First, if everyone performed their best in all walks of life, could you even begin to imagine what the world would look like? If all were determined to provide only the best of service to others, wouldn't that be amazing? Of course, it would be. Imagine that every time you ordered your #1 combo at the fast-food restaurant, the food was always hot, the drink was never flat, and you always had plenty of ketchup and napkins. So, why do some people decide to give less than their best? Yes, sometimes the answer could be tied to sheer laziness, but deeper than that, the answer is nestled in our understanding of the unpopular moral law. When people do not comprehend the consequences of their actions, it's easier to care less about doing their best. Not near as often as in our recent past, but if the guy or gal responsible for getting your order correct and in a timely manner understood they could be written up, or ever worse, fired for not doing their best, they may be inclined to work a little harder to satisfy the customer.

As poor an analogy as it may be, if we view God as our Commander in Chief while aboard the sub, or as a customer at our restaurant we serve in, we would do well to consider the consequences of not doing our best. Ultimately, He is the boss. He is in a position of authority and our job is to do our

SUB-MISSION: The Silent Service

best to satisfy His desires and follow His laws and instructions without complaint or question.

Some draw a hard line and refuse to break the laws of the land, following all speed limits, not playing loud music after 9:00 PM, and wearing safety glasses while mowing their lawn. Many of these same people, while faithful to the laws of the land, are anything but faithful to moral law of God.

To be faithful to moral law, we must first understand exactly what it is and where it comes from. Of course, some will argue that this is not an objective truth but rather a subjective opinion. However, to the Christian, and even more so, the Apostolic Christian, there should be no confusion here. The objective truth is, there is a God (Commander in Chief), and He is good. Thus, God is the standard of moral law. He has, from the beginning, always given His best. God by His nature cannot do any less than what is best as He is all good, the very definition of good.

From the beginning, or scripturally speaking, the book of beginnings (Genesis), God has given His best. He spoke His creative Word amid utter chaos and prepared a place, a good place for His ultimate prized possession to exist: you and me. He could have kept us in the dark, literally, but rather, He chose to shed a Heavenly light upon the face of the new earth to illuminate our surroundings. Why? Because He always gives His best. He could have created only the seas and land, void of plants, trees, and animals, but He didn't. Why? Because He always gives His best. He could have smitten

Adam and Eve for their disobedience, banishing them from the face of the earth, forever to exist in a devil's hell, but He didn't. He chose mercy and forgiveness, clothing them to cover their nakedness and shame. Why? Again, because He always gives His best.

We could literally walk through all 39 books of the Old Testament, and 27 from the New Testament, giving example after example of God giving His best and never withholding what is ultimately good for His creation, but time will simply not allow it in this setting. However, I will provide one more example of God leading by example in giving His best as I remember Jesus' cross on Calvary's hill.

Oh, what a thought! Jesus, the mighty God, manifest in the flesh, hanging on a tree that was a product of His own spoken Word. He was crucified by His own children, ultimately for simply claiming to be their long-awaited Messiah and Savior, the one of whom the prophets of old said would come. What an image that floods my mind as I think about that great and terrible day when the God of all creation lay His life down for His friends, giving His best, His life!

So, how about it, why not your best? Why, when God bankrupted Heaven to offer us salvation, do we in return, give less than our best? While there is much that could be said in response to this, I submit to you that it is a moral issue. When one does not value the standard of moral goodness (God), they are not compelled to follow in the footsteps of the arbiter of moral goodness. Therefore, people like you and I can comfortably give less than our best and still go to sleep without giving it a second thought. We have become numb to God's example of moral goodness, and it is quite the shame.

I want to care. I want it to affect me when I do not give my best. I want to be convicted when I have deliberately performed a mediocre job. Let it not be said of me that I only did the bare minimum, just enough to get by. God has equipped you and me for so much more. God has blessed me to be able to give 100% to the building of His kingdom. God gave His all. Why should I, being made in His image, not be required to do the same.

As it pertains to life beneath the surface of the sea, aboard our nuclear submarine, giving our best is not optional. One submariner giving anything less than their best could be to the detriment of the whole crew. If just one crew member does not pull their weight, does not step up to the plate when something goes wrong, or does not always perform at the highest level, it could cost everyone their lives. The success of the submarine and all those aboard doesn't just depend on one of the submariners, regardless of their position or authority. From architects to engineers to craftsmen such as welders, electricians, and plumbers, all the way to the very sailors who operate the boat, all have a great responsibility to do their best.

One design miscalculation, one improper weld, one bad switch or seal, or one bad sailor could cause an unfathomable amount of loss. Every (t) must be crossed and every (i) must be dotted. There is literally no room for anything less than the best from each one of those who have a hand in both the design, construction, and operation of a submarine. Talk about pressure…

Okay, let's do it. Let's talk about pressure. Each 10 meters (33 feet) of depth puts another atmosphere (1 bar, 14.7 psi kPa) of pressure on the hull, so at 300 meters (1,000 feet), the hull is withstanding thirty atmospheres (30 bar, 441 psi, 3,000 kPa) of water pressure. That's a lot of pressure. The pressure hull is designed to expand, and contract based on the outside pressure.

> *"In God's sacred school of submission and brokenness, why are there so few students? Because all students in this school must suffer much pain. And as you might guess, it is often the unbroken ruler (whom God sovereignly picks) who metes out the pain. David was once a student in this school, and Saul was God's chosen way to crush David." Gene Edwards*
>
> *– A Tale of Three Kings*

Aboard our submarine in the lower deck, you see a red string spanning the width of the pressure hull. You hesitantly ask the question, "What's that for?" One of the mechanics—a veteran submariner standing in the corner with a smirk on his face—

SUB-MISSION: The Silent Service

pipes up and explains, "That string is a visual representation of the pressure the hull is under at any given time. The tighter it is, the less pressure we are under. The looser it is, the more pressure against the hull. Hence the name, pressure hull." As the words were proceeding out of his mouth, it dawned on both you and me—as we took notice of the swoop in the line—that we were under a lot of pressure.

Immediately my mind started racing, thinking about the welds that were laid in the shipyard as this submarine was being built. I thought about the inspection process and wondered what if the inspector had a bad day or was distracted during his final report before signing off. What if someone didn't do their best, I wondered. I hope and pray that they took their jobs seriously, because I am the one down here with this dumb red string.

Do you see the importance of everyone doing their best? Obviously, none of us can perform consistently without failing from time to time. We all fall short in one way or another. But when it comes to living a submitted life, one must accept the weight of responsibility, understanding the potential cost if we do not do our absolute best. Think of it this way, when you begin a life of submission, you are subjecting yourself to another. You are opting for silence when everything in you desires to be heard. If you do not give your best, you put at stake not only your own self but also the relationships that are built upon your life of submission.

Consider a cadet who is submitted to the XO;

respect and obedience mean a great deal. Not only does the XO expect to be given due respect and for direct orders to be followed, but it is demanded from the top down. We learned this in basic training. Even if you find fault in the individual, as a cadet, respect should be given to the office and rank of an XO. Even when it's hard to respect the man or woman in the position, you must respect the position. Success honors authority.

It is not uncommon aboard a Naval submarine to see the captain of the boat, an officer, or someone else in a position of authority helping with the day-to-day operations. Those in authority understand the principle of teamwork and do not mind getting their hands dirty from time to time. At the same time, those who are in positions of greater responsibility must keep in mind the need they have for each crew member. The XO, as important as his position is, simply cannot do it all, nor should he or she try. Everyone has their limits, and everyone should do their very best within those limits.

Let's look at this point considering the house of God. Is it acceptable for some saints to be bench warmers, standing idly by, afraid to get their hands dirty while a core group does all the work? Absolutely not. Sadly, the fact remains that within most churches, you will find a small handful of people who do 95% of the work while most weekly congregants are content with doing less than their best.

Understandably, some people have more liberty to help with most, if not all projects within

SUB-MISSION: THE SILENT SERVICE

the local church. A church may have several retired saints who are able to come and go as they please, while others may be limited by their work schedules, family dynamics, finances, etc. But one thing I have learned is this: with whatever you have been given, if you give it back to God, He can multiply it and use it for His Kingdom. You may not have a lot of time but if you use what time you do have for His Kingdom, He will bless you for it. You may not have excess funds available, but if you will take what funds you do have and be faithful with them, God will bless you. One thing is for sure, you cannot out give God!

When you understand who it is that you are giving to and why you are giving in the first place, you will soon learn, if you do not withhold your best from Him, He will not withhold His best from you. So, why not your best? The question seems a little more reasonable now that we understand that God will not ask us to do anything that He is not willing to do. He can ask for all from us because He first gave all. He can ask us to give of our time because He stepped into time on our behalf. He can ask us to give of our finances because He is the source of all good gifts. We serve a mighty good God, friends.

If you will put God first and make Him a priority, you will begin to see just how able He is to provide for you. Often, the problem is that we do not see God moving in a certain area of our lives. That is because He has not been made Lord of that area of our lives. If you are having marital problems, could it be because He is not Lord of your marriage? If you are having financial problems, could it be because He is not Lord of your finances? This principle can be applied in most areas of our lives.

God did not choose you because you were qualified. He did not choose you because of your talent. God does not look at the outward appearance of an individual, but rather at their heart.

> *But the LORD said unto Samuel, Look not on his countenance, or on the height of his stature; because I have refused him: for the LORD seeth not as man seeth; for man looketh on the outward appearance, but the LORD looketh on the heart.*
>
> *1 Samuel 16:7 KJV*

God is more interested in whether you are submitted. Are you submitted to Him as your Commander in Chief? Are you submitted to your pastor and spiritual leadership? Are you submitted to the Word of God? Do you do your best? If the answer to these questions is yes, then God can promote you within His Kingdom. If the answer to any of these questions is no, God can still use you, but He will first take you to the bottom to rid you of any pride you may have.

Throughout the Word of God, we see a recurring pattern: the last shall be first, He uses the weak to lead the strong, my strength is made perfect

SUB-MISSION: The Silent Service

in weakness. We can see how God can use opposites to fulfill His will. Therefore, we should not think it strange when God takes us to the bottom, a place of humility and complete submission, in order to exalt us. As a matter of fact, I would say that one cannot fully realize their potential in Christ until they have fully submitted to Him in every way, even the most painful. Let's commit to giving our best to Him starting now.

> *"I did not recruit extraordinary people. I recruited people who had extraordinary potential-and then I trained them."*
>
> *Admiral Rickover*

SUB-MISSION: The Silent Service

4
ANTI-SUBMISSION

Within the scope of a submariner's life and commitment to the call of duty aboard a nuclear submarine is the realization that death is never far away. At a moment's notice, things can go from test dives, fire drills, and meatloaf for dinner, to DEFCON 1 (nuclear warfare). Without warning, an enemy sub can hurl multiple torpedoes toward our sub in an act of modern-day warfare. We must always be ready for when danger strikes; there will be no time to get ready.

Torpedoes are the preferred method of modern-day warfare. ASW (anti-submarine warfare) is always at the forefront of our minds below the surface of the deep. Not long ago, one of the major potential threats submarines faced was known as a depth charge. Less popular now due to advances in ASW, a depth charge was a unique weapon designed to destroy a submarine by being dropped into the water nearby and then detonating, subjecting the sub to a powerful and destructive hydraulic shock. These depth charges would be dropped by surface ships, patrol aircraft, and helicopters. Sea-floor mines also posed a major threat to those who live aboard a submarine.

Similarly, one of the more common attacks of our enemy is to attack you while you are dived (submitted). While he cannot touch you without first receiving permission from God, the enemy would love to send a spiritual depth charge into your vicinity, causing a shockwave in your life. Often, his attacks are not physical or even tangible, but they are simply scare tactics, designed to incite fear and chaos. Remember, he has no power over you; he cannot destroy you. Bishop Jack Cunningham once powerfully said, "If the devil could kill you, you'd be dead, but he can't do it. He can't do it!"

While there is always the potential of an enemy attack for those in the silent service, likewise, there is an ever-present threat to those of us who plunge headlong into a life of submission. Yes, in some respects, there is safety in submission, and we will discuss that later in the book. However, we must also be aware that when we enlist into the silent service—a life of submission—we automatically become a target. Sure, we could safely spend our days living life above the surface, but those days would never satisfy the deep desire within our hearts to serve and protect.

Much like the Navies of our world, be it the United States Navy, Russian Navy, Republic of China Navy, etc., all preparing themselves for local or global war by investing in their own version of the silent service, we too must immerse ourselves in the deep waters of submission to ready ourselves for a war. But who exactly are we at war with: China, Russia, Bangladesh? No, we have been thrust

SUB-MISSION: THE SILENT SERVICE

headlong into a battle that is far superior to even the likes of WWI (15-22 million deaths), WWII (50-56 million deaths), or even the impending WWIII (1/3 of the world's population will be destroyed).

However, our war is vastly different in that we are not in a battle with another country. In fact, our war is not even of this world. As born-again believers as outlined in John 3:5, we are automatically drafted into a battle that has been underway for many millennia. This battle is unlike any other that we are familiar with, as this is a spiritual battle, held in a realm that is otherworldly. This battle cannot be fought with fists, guns, or torpedoes, for "the weapons of our warfare are not carnal, but they are mighty through God to the pulling down of strongholds" (2 Corinthians 10:4 KJV).

So, if not fists, guns, or nuclear torpedoes, what then do we house in our arsenal to fight in this spiritual battle? How do we wage war against an invisible enemy whose sole purpose in life is to destroy those who are now, and who will be in the future, submitted? How might we fend off those who are anti submission? The answer may not be what you are thinking. In fact, it may well be the exact opposite of one's intuition. The way to fight the one who is fighting you as you try to submit, is to submit even more: go deeper, become more silent for longer periods of time. Remember, as a submariner, our job is to remain unseen. When we are unseen, we have the advantage.

Do you remember The Turtle, the first American war submarine used during the American revolution? Designed by David Bushnell in 1775, this sub could be submerged up to 20 feet for a half hour at a time. While this does not seem very impressive to us in comparison to today's capabilities, in 1775, this was an amazing feat. But like all things, there is a need and expectancy to do more, go higher, go further. A half hour was hardly enough time to sneak up on the British warships in the New York harbor, attempting to affix explosives to them in an act of war. More time was needed. Bushnell just needed to stay dived for longer and possibly, he would have been more successful.

The first goal of the enemy is to keep you from submitting in the first place. If he can keep you in his sight, visible and at bay, you pose much less of a threat to him and his kingdom. However, if you can ever learn submission, disappearing into the depths of selflessness, you gain the advantage. Remember, you are a lot more dangerous to your adversary when he doesn't know where you are. Under the surface of the deep, for us submariners, life is a lot like a game of cat and mouse.

While The Turtle remained unsuccessful in its attempts to bring down an enemy ship, in part, due to its limited diving time capacity of a half hour, its runner up, The Nautilus, in 1800 proved to be quite the improvement at four and a half hours dived. You can follow the history of improvements made to submarines year after year, and one thing always seemed to be a priority: the length of time dived. Everyone seemed to understand the benefits of being submerged for the longest period possible.

SUB-MISSION: The Silent Service

From a half hour to a few hours. From a few hours to a couple of days. From days to weeks and weeks to months, engineers have learned how to design and stock their boat with enough food, fresh water, and oxygen to live a life beneath the sea for an extended amount of time. Modern day submarines can easily stay dived for four plus months, only surfacing to restock their spent supplies, just to dive again. In light of this, let me say that nothing will prove to be more valuable than you submitting your life. But to what, or to whom should we be submitting? I am glad you asked.

Back to the story: We stood by quietly as we saw a young and inexperienced submariner learn a life lesson during his first week aboard the sub. He was sure to never disrespect the XO, understanding his rank and position. He gave due respect to him and the chief of the boat. But when it came to his peers, the chef in the kitchen, the sonar specialist, and pretty much anyone else he met, this guy was anything but submitted.

It's not that we demanded respect or held some prestigious position that would demand such, but aboard a submarine for months at a time, there is a profound awareness of the need each submariner has for their brothers and sisters aboard. Most submariners show respect because we understand that each one, the XO, chief of the boat, the sonar specialist, and even the chef, all have given up their freedom and their families to allow those above the surface to live their lives worry free.

First and foremost, we are to submit to the

Commander in Chief (God). He deserves our best as He has given His best to us. When you submit to God, you are submitting to His will for your life. You understand that you are not your own, and whatever he asks of you, you will gladly comply because you are submitted. To be submitted to God as Commander in Chief, we will be sure to yield to Him and His will. We will allow Him to precede our every move and decision as He is the one whom we are subject to.

Second, we should be submitted to those in positions of authority in the natural realm. Of course, the Word of God teaches us to obey the laws of the land, and I support being in submission to our police officers and law givers, but even more importantly, spiritually, we must be willing to submit to those in positions of authority within the body of Christ.

Every member of the local church should be in submission to their pastor and to the leadership. Again, this is not about ego or slave mentality. It is about defeating the enemy of our soul: pride. If you cannot be submitted to your leadership, what makes you think you can be submitted to God Himself? You and I both know it simply will not happen that way. Your level of submission to God will very much depend on your level of submission to your leadership.

A lot of the time, the reason why we are willing to submit to God but have a hard time submitting to leadership is because God has no flaws, but sometimes the flaws of our leadership are visible. While it's not fair to the leadership, understanding

SUB-MISSION: The Silent Service

that "pastor" or "preacher" does not mean "perfect," we feel as though we cannot submit ourselves to someone we know is equally as flawed as we are. When this is the case, we do not yet understand how submission works. Biblical submission is not based on merit or what seems fair. For Biblical proof of this, study the relationship between King Saul and David.

As a submariner, with millions of lives on the line, we simply cannot afford to fall into this anti sub trap. Our XO's (spiritual leaders) are often initially viewed as untouchable, without fault, and some would even say, perfect. After all, XOs tend to dress a certain way, carry themselves a certain way, and even talk a certain way. There is an intimidation that comes alongside their welcoming speech as you join them on their boat.

XO's do not have to state that they are in a position of authority as is obvious by their very demeanor. As young submariners, we understand our place and rank and are sure not to speak unless spoken to. It goes without saying, the newbies are to simply stay quiet and do our jobs. If you are still making the spiritual connections here with the XO playing the role of your pastor, it may seem that I am painting pastors in a bad light. However, I reiterate the fact that these are often simply initial observations, which are often misconstrued.

Given the opportunity to lead by example, a good XO, while he may appear to be bigger than life, will admit that he is no different than we are, human, except for experience. I don't know about you, but

I am thankful that my XO has some experience that I do not have. I am thankful that this is not his first sub mission, and I can learn a thing or two if I can lay aside my initial desire to cast judgement and pretend that rank doesn't matter.

The reason this realization is paramount is because without rank and experience, submission cannot exist. And where submission does not exist, arrogance and pride will thrive. We submariners would be so focused on ourselves, jockeying for position, vying for power, that we would probably miss the new activity on our sonar screen, an enemy threat that opposes our very existence. While we are focused on fighting with one another, the enemy have set their sights on us, and now we are in grave danger. Anti-submission is not just a difference in opinion, it is treason. If you are not supporting your leadership, you are attempting to defeat your leadership. If you are attempting to defeat your leadership, you are a rogue submariner who has joined the anti-sub enemy.

Forced to stop fighting amongst ourselves due to an aggravated enemy sub, we turn our attention to the sonar screens to find a torpedo headed straight at us. It is at this moment that everyone forgets their personal agendas, and the crew is unified to save the boat from a direct hit. The XO receives an update from the sonar personnel and immediately makes the call, "dive! dive! dive!" Without question or hesitation, each crew member does their part to further dive the boat.

The chief of the boat makes the final call

SUB-MISSION: The Silent Service

as everyone is uncertain of their fate, "Brace for impact." In this moment, no one aboard the sub is concerned about their rank or the flaws of their peers. Nobody is standing idle, gossiping about the leadership, questioning their decisions. No, at this moment, our life preserving instinct is to simply submit.

As each of our lives flash before our eyes, and each second seems like an eternity, we wait to see if our actions and inactions will prove to be a fatal blow. And just when we thought our lives were all over with, we realized that the torpedo had missed us. A miracle had truly occurred as it could have only been a couple of feet away from a direct hit. The crew has a moment of relief as each one of us cracks a smile with our eyes wide open in disbelief. While us new and inexperienced submariners come to realize what just happened, it dawns on us that had the XO not made the command when he did, we would have all perished.

It was not the rank or title of the XO that saved the boat, it was experience. That split second decision to dive was the result of many years of being submerged beneath the surface of the sea, fighting those who are anti sub. Because he had been in similar situations before, and we had not, the XO was able to thrive under pressure while the rest of us would have caved. It was a miracle!

"The key to the miraculous is submission!"

—Billy Cole

You and I need to learn to trust and obey our leadership regardless of our opinion. The Scripture is clear in teaching us that God places leaders over the saints and gives them direction to watch out for our souls. "Obey them that have the rule over you, and submit yourselves: for they watch for your souls…" (Hebrews 13:17 KJV). As long as my spiritual leader is living a consecrated life, lining up with the Word of God as best he can, then I am obligated to trust and obey his leadership.

The remainder of that verse says, "…as they that must give an account, that they may do it with joy, and not with grief: for that is unprofitable for you" (Hebrews 13:17 KJV). Understand, the bulk of the weight of responsibility is not on the saint but is on the leader. My job as a saint in this context is to be submitted to my leadership. My spiritual leader's job is to watch out for the souls of all the saints that God has trusted into his care, however many there may be.

When your spiritual leader stands before God in judgement, he will have to give an account for every word that he ever spoke into your life, good or bad. Your spiritual leader will be held accountable for having preached the gospel of Jesus Christ to you. The leader stands the chance of having your blood on his hands if he does not tell you the truth. It's obvious that the leader has a great deal of responsibility, and this role in the Kingdom of God should not be taken lightly.

However, the spiritual leader is not responsible for our response. How we respond to the Word of

SUB-MISSION: The Silent Service

God when it comes into our lives has no bearing on how he will be judged. That weight of responsibility falls on us, the recipient. We, too, will have to stand before God in judgement and will have to give an account as to how we responded to the Word of God.

> *Therefore to him that knoweth to do good, and doeth it not, to him it is sin.*
>
> *James 4:17*

You will never fully submit to a leader that you cannot trust. That is not to say that you cannot be submitted to God and do what is right. Take for example, David and King Saul. King Saul was the leader, and David was to be in submission to him. As King Saul became jealous of the praises of David having killed tens of thousands more in battle than the king, Saul became enraged and sought to kill David.

Through several attempts on King Saul's part to kill David, Saul quickly fell into the trap of self-preservation, ignoring the voice of the man of God in his life: Samuel. Saul became drunk on pride and power. When one allows themself to travel down this unforgiving road of self-indulgence, harm comes, not only to said person but also to the undeserving. Saul's pride was hurt, and as the adage goes, "hurt people, hurt people."

David, a man after God's own heart—one who always showed love and respect to leadership—was now being hunted by his own king, Saul. David, rather than falling prey to his own fleshly desires to defend himself, chose to flee from Saul. David found himself on the run, hiding in obscure places such as forests and caves. With Saul and his mighty men hot on David's trail, I can only imagine how David must have felt, abandoned, rejected, fearful.

Many people, when thinking about David running for his life, imagine him being scared to death of what Saul would do to him if he were to be caught. I, on the other hand, tend to view David a little differently than most. I do agree that David was scared, but I don't believe that David feared what Saul would do to him. I believe that David feared what he would do to Saul if he (David) gave in to his fleshly desires, taking vengeance into his own hands.

After all, this is the same David that slew a lion and a bear with his bare hands. This is the same David that offered to fight the biggest, baddest warrior of the Philistine army: the giant, Goliath. David was known as a mighty man of valor who had killed tens of thousands of warriors, much more than Saul ever killed. From my point of view, David thought, if I don't run away from this situation, I may give in to the warrior inside of me, and who knows what I will do to Saul.

David's respect for the position that Saul held would not let him stay and fight. David was submitted and knew that if God allowed Saul to remain king, he (David) could not lay a hand on God's anointed. David ran to protect the king even when the king

SUB-MISSION: The Silent Service

sought to kill David. This is the true sign of a submitted life, even when it's hard to respect and submit to the spiritual leader, you choose to respect and submit to the office of the spiritual leader.

Those who are anti submission are not few, but many. In the natural realm, there will be pawns of Satan who will try to deter you from living a life of submission. Likewise, in the spirit realm, there are a host of fallen angels whose sole purpose and desire is to keep you from submitting. The opposers know that if you will learn to submit to God and to your spiritual leadership, like David, you will be exalted in due time. Not exalted by human hands to gain glory in this life but exalted by the hand of God to bring glory to His name.

> *"There is no virtue solely in authority, obedience, unity, or submission in and of themselves. For example, it is no virtue for one to obey someone in authority who orders that person to do anything contrary to the Scriptures. What benefit is there in unity if those unified are united in rebellion or in unbiblical practices? Individuals can unite themselves in crime or other sins. Submission to those who would lead us into iniquity has no virtue whatsoever. So, the virtue then is not in authority, obedience, unity, or submission. The virtue of these is in the greater noble cause to which they join us. Absent*

that noble cause, there is no virtue."

*Integrity: Principles of Christian
Ethics, Richard M. Davis*

5
CRUSH DEPTH

During our time in basic training at the Naval Submarine School, they taught us many things. We learned the basic skills required to operate the complex equipment that fills a modern submarine. Also, we learned to deal with such emergencies as onboard flooding and fire. Finally, we learned the more advanced procedures and specialties such as active/passive sonar use and nuclear weapons training.

While everything you learn in the Naval Submarine School has a direct impact on your career and ultimately your life abord a submarine, there are certain things that you learn that you don't soon forget. One of the topics of discussion during our training was called "crush depth." When the teacher began to discuss the harrowing details of crush depth, there fell upon the room a heavy quietness.

Everyone in attendance that day seemed to have lost their zeal for their future life as a submariner as we all realized the possibility of the catastrophic. But most of the men and women of the Navy are not quick to back out when things get hard. It's in their DNA; they won't settle for anything less than fulfilling their life's dream, their calling. While talking about the hazards of reaching the crush depth is serious business, we assume the risk and proceed in our training to plumb the depths of the deep.

The teacher explained that all subs are given specific depth ratings during the design process. This is to ensure the safety of all submariners as well as the sub itself. From it the designers calculate the thickness of the metal hull, the boat's displacement, and many other related factors. Once the sub receives its design depth rating, it can go on to receive its test depth rating which is the maximum depth at which a submarine is permitted to operate under normal peacetime circumstances. The test depth is set at two-thirds (0.66) of the design depth for US Navy submarines.

Once we had passed all the particulars, we finally received the information that everyone really wanted to know. Exactly what is a crush depth and what happens to the boat and its passengers at the crush depth? The answer is not for the faint of heart. As you may surmise from the name, crush depth, something probably crushes. But what? The boat? The people? Yes, that is exactly what happens. There is a point that all submarines can reach at which the outside pressure becomes too much for the boat and the materials that make up the boat can no longer sustain the pressure, leaving one final option: implosion.

Above the surface of the sea, most humanity is familiar with explosions, but few have experience with implosion. An explosion is a violent and destructive shattering or blowing apart of something, as is caused by a bomb. An implosion, on the other hand, is an instance of something collapsing violently inward upon itself. While both are very destructive in their own right, the likelihood of an explosion as opposed to an implosion for a submarine is small.

When a submarine reaches its actual crush depth, it implodes as the extreme outside pressure causes the hull to collapse in on itself, crushing everything in the process. There are several examples of a submarine imploding throughout history. Notably, the USS Thresher, which imploded off the coast of Cape Cod in April 1963, killing its 129 crewmembers, making it the deadliest submarine accident in U.S. history.

Later, in November 2017, the Argentine submarine, ARA San Juan, went missing off the coast of Argentina while on a training exercise, killing all 44 crew members on board. And most recently, as I was writing this book, the world's news outlets began covering the story of Titan, a submersible belonging to OceanGate that imploded during a tourist expedition to view the wreck of the Titanic. This most recent incident killed all 5 passengers aboard.

While submarine implosions are nothing new, they are always catastrophic and call for new safety measures and SOP's to be written. One would assume that safety is always the top priority, especially in this line of work, but that is not always the case. For example, the creator of Titan, Stockton Rush III, was encouraged by a group of engineers to seek certification of the Titan by a safety agency. He declined and replied, "Regulation would stifle innovation."

While all these examples are horrible tragedies, and I do not attempt to make light of the loss of life, I believe there is a great lesson to be learned here. To learn this lesson, we will have to use our spiritual periscope to view things from a submerged perspective. We must take the lessons learned from the natural and apply them to our submitted lives to fully see the effects of a spiritual crush depth. While in the natural world, a crush depth is a dangerous realm that all seek to avoid, but in a spiritual sense, the crush depth is exactly what we are after: a place where our egotistic will is crushed.

Spiritually speaking, when we enter a life of submission, we are ever in pursuit of the crush depth, even if it's not at first realized. At first, you may not mind the beautiful scenery as you wade into the ankle-deep waters of submission. In fact, this is where a lot of saints tend to spend most of their time, simply because this area can be fun. Living for God can be a good time. You may enjoy coming to church, fellowshipping with your brothers and sisters in the Lord. You may love to sing, dance, and shout as the musicians sing your favorite song. But one thing is certain, ankle-deep water doesn't satisfy the soul for long.

After the fun has been had and there is no other place you would rather be than in the house of the Lord, you realize that the ankle-deep waters are leaving you wanting more. What would happen if

SUB-MISSION: The Silent Service

you waded out a little further, maybe up to your knees? We are sure that deeper waters would equate to more fun, right? Well, kind of. When you get out to knee-deep water, you realize that you can still have fun, but the waves tend to knock you off balance. You still have a smile on your face, and your hair isn't even wet. Knee-deep water is not suitable for unattended toddlers but is mostly safe for youth and especially us adults. Knee-deep water is still child's play at this point. You don't have to be very serious at this point, so we wade out a little further in search of something a little more age appropriate, waters up to our thighs.

Here in water up to our thighs, we realize that the waves are taking the upper hand. They are often stronger than we are and can even knock us over completely, washing us back up on the shore. Have you ever thought about the weight of a wave? Well, consider this: According to physicists, a breaking wave can apply a pressure of between 250-6,000 pounds per square foot (1,220-29,294 kilograms per square meter), depending on its height. So, imagine a 20-inch (50 centimeters) thick wave lip, only 3.2 feet wide, in a summer, three-foot wave; the total weight would be a solid 500 kilograms (1,100 pounds).

Once we get beyond the breaking waves, we are in deep enough water to swim in, to dive in. These waters can be enjoyable also, but they pose greater threats to those of us who venture out into them. Anyone who enters these deeper waters must first know how to swim. But even if you know how to swim, you must consider things outside of your control, such as rip currents, sharks, your level of exhaustion, etc. The deeper you go, the more pressure mounts, also.

You may not fully understand nor like the mounting pressure that comes with diving into the deep waters of submission. However, the more pressure you feel, the more you can be sure you are going where few have gone before. Pressure reveals many things and one of those things is progress. When a submarine dives, there are no windows, so you cannot look outside to see where you are or how deep you have gone. The only way for a submariner to know their depth is to have a working gauge. The gauge reveals the active pressure against it, so you know how deep you have dived. This is important for many reasons.

One of the reasons why a depth gauge is so important is for ASW avoidance. We want to be deep enough where our position is not easily known. Remember, if the enemy cannot find us, and we know their position, we are winning. The second reason why a depth gauge is so important is to keep us aware of the crush depth. Naturally, we need to always be aware of this zone to avoid it, but spiritually speaking, this is our target zone. We are in pursuit of the crush depth of our own will and fleshly desire; a place where pride cannot survive.

While pressure reveals progress, it also reveals weaknesses. Every weld, bolt, rivet, and seal are put to the test as we dive into the deep. If just one of these items fail to perform, it could result

SUB-MISSION: THE SILENT SERVICE

in a catastrophe. Every one of these areas must be thoroughly inspected before a safe dive can be achieved. We cannot take for granted that all is well and there is no need for inspection. If there is a weak spot, a broken seal or fractured weld, the mounting pressure will be sure to make it known. Don't be surprised as you dive into a life of submission to find out that you have a few leaks here and there. This does not mean that you are not capable of diving. It simply means that you need to do some surface work before going deeper.

Once all the surface flaws are dealt with, we can dive to depths we have never been to before. It's a lonely journey as there are few people willing to do what it takes to traverse the depths of submission. But one thing is for sure, you are not alone. Even when you feel like you are alone and no one can relate to where you are, there is another submariner there, going through exactly what you are going through. Don't fall into the trap of isolation. Submariners stick together. Together, we are one. What we do down here is invaluable. It takes a special person to survive down here. It takes a special person to place the well-being of others above themselves. That is what submission is all about.

> *"...submission is not separate from mission. Submission is the underground version of mission. Submission is to mission what roots are to a tree. Your mission is worth nothing unless there is submission."*
> —Joel Urshan

As we endeavor to reach our crush depth, we realize that the pressure of these deep waters is affecting every aspect of our lives. We can see the effects of atmospheric pressure from every angle the deeper we go. Have you ever tried to be in submission to someone and failed? I have. On the surface it seems simple enough: just submit. But I learned that to truly be submitted is not at all about the other person but is completely about me. Let me explain...

At first, I thought that being in submission to someone else was only a result of who they were and the position they held. Boy, was I wrong. Of course, we should give honor to those in positions of authority and leadership just as we expressed earlier when talking about the XO. But true submission is far deeper than any position or title. Submission is about one's self-identity. It's about revealing your own weaknesses and allowing them to be crushed by the weight of your own selflessness. There are levels of submission that correlate to the depth of water we are in.

Ankle-deep water reveals that there is more of us above the water than beneath. We are easily visible to everyone around, and for the most part, it's all about having fun and being in control. Ankle-deep water is the safe zone, the farthest you can get from the crush depth. This shallow depth of water allows us to feel the water but not be moved by it. We are technically in it but not submitted to it. This is also the easiest depth of water to remove ourself from. If we don't like something, just simply walk out of the water with little effort, and we have completely removed ourself from any trace of submission. Ankle-deep water, while it may not cause much pressure, is the most dangerous depth we can be in.

Knee-deep water is a little more challenging, but we remain in control. There are plenty of opportunities for fun and play. Knee-deep water, while able to move us, doesn't conceal us. We are still very visible to everyone around, and again, we can easily remove ourself from the water, never fully submitting to anything or anyone.

Spiritually speaking, many people in the church today are in knee-deep water. They wade out just far enough to be a little spiritual but tend to show more flesh than submission. The occasional wave brushes them, and for a moment, they are a little deeper, but at the end of the day, they are not even swimming, allowing the water to take them. They are still in full control, standing on their own two feet.

Those who stand in water up to their thigh are those who are about half in and half out. They are not submerged but they know the power of the water. These individuals tend to like the idea of power but resist pressure. They know that if they wade out any further, the power they feel may turn into pressure, leading to a pride-crushing depth that they are not comfortable with. At times, those who stand in thigh-deep water are in control, but occasionally the water does have its way with them, knocking them over. As mentioned before, these people tend to be washed back to shore, starting over where they began, in ankle-deep water. If you never commit to diving deep into the waters of submission that are over your head, you will likely default back to the desire of your flesh.

Then there are those who will go where few others have gone before: the depths of the unknown. When you get in over your head, you lose your control and are subject to the desires of the water, or in this case, the one who controls the water, the Commander in Chief (Jesus). When you give in to your spiritual desire to go deeper, you forfeit your flesh, your pride, and your control for what is ultimately not seen: true submission. You can no longer easily walk out of the water, defaulting back to your old ways. The fun in the shallows and the power of the waves turns into pressure, and it is coming in from every angle. It's not comfortable, but comfort is not why you came out this deep. You came out here for something different, something that you could not get on the shore: submission.

Learning to live a life of submission is going to cost you something. You cannot afford the lessons learned in the deep while remaining in shallow pockets. You must make up in your mind, I desire more than what I have been walking in. The norm can no longer satisfy you if you are to wade out into the waters of submission.

True submission is ultimately found at crush depth, the place where the desires of your carnality cannot survive. Getting to this place is not a walk in the park. In fact, it is a dive in the deep. You

SUB-MISSION: The Silent Service

must disappear. You must decrease so that God can have His perfect way with you. You must allow the pressure to rid you of all your pride and self-preservation. You must give in to the Spirit, killing the flesh, to gain the supernatural.

Allow me to be clear. When I speak of disappearing, I am not implying that you run away from your church, your family, or your friends. When I speak of killing the flesh, I am not insinuating that you do harm to yourself. These expressions are meant to be taken spiritually. To disappear spiritually is to stop making everything about you. You do not have to be the center of attention all the time. You do not need to be the one in the spotlight. As a matter of fact, Jesus should be the only one in the spotlight. When you are trying to defeat the enemy that is pride, you need to learn to take the focus off you and place it on others. God did not save you for you, He saved you for others.

Killing the flesh is a reference to the fleshly desires that we all must battle against. The flesh seeks the benefit of the flesh. We must kill the desire of the flesh by starving the flesh, not feeding it by fueling our own pride with self-exaltation.

"It does not matter how much you pray, even if you pray in tongues more than in English. If you are not submitted to the Word, the Spirit, and your pastor; then you have disqualified yourself from being truly used by God. If you

are used, you will be in danger because you do not have the covering safety of submission. Boundaries or fences are not meant for bondage in the Kingdom of God; they are meant for protection."

Mike McGurk - The Conquered Campus

You will know when you have reached the level of true submission that God desires for you to be in. You will know because there are signs that will follow. When you reach the crush depth, your personal agenda will transition into the agenda of others. You will not pray for yourself and your benefit, but you will pray for others and for God to prosper them. When you enter the crush depth, you are less concerned with leading and more concerned with following. You will become increasingly aware of the pains of others and less aware of your own discomfort. Submission awakens you to the fact that it is no longer about you. It is about the Kingdom of God.

The crush depth is not meant to kill the spirit but is designed to kill the flesh, the pride of the flesh. There is an easy way to tell if you are not truly living a submitted life, and that is whether or not the pride of your flesh is still living. That is not to say that you will never have to battle the flesh again. In fact, you must continually live in the crush depth to ensure that the desires of your flesh remain in check. Just as entering the crush depth will prove to be a fatal blow to the pride in your life, leaving the crush depth—surfacing to the shores of carnality—

SUB-MISSION: THE SILENT SERVICE

will resurrect the pride in your life. Stay focused on submission and do not be satisfied with just playing in the shallow waters. God is calling you into the deep, into the crush depth.

6
SURFACING

While we do not want to surface, returning to the shores of carnality (as previously discussed in the last chapter), there is a time when surfacing is necessary. Throughout our time in the Navy as submariners, beginning in basic training, coming aboard this nuclear-capable sub, we have learned so much. We have learned the art of reconnaissance, where we were taught to see but not be seen. We learned why it is necessary to always give our best and leave nothing undone to preserve not only our lives, but the lives of everyone else. We have learned to be cognizant of those who oppose our very existence: to keep a watchful eye on them that are anti-submission. And lastly, we have learned the pros and cons of the crush depth.

Of course, naturally speaking, submarines must surface every few months for several reasons. They must restock their food supply, perform repairs, release some submariers from duty, and bring some new submariners aboard. However, spiritually speaking, once you obtain a life of submission, and you have reached your crush depth, you should not surface until your mission is complete. After all, there is nothing to surface for. Your fleshly desires are dead, and your way of living has forever changed. To surface now would be a great disservice not only to yourself but to your fellow submariners, your XO, and most importantly, the Commander in Chief.

You are not interested in returning to the shallow waters that always left you wanting more. You will not be satisfied with returning to the childish games in the ankle-deep or knee-deep waters. Those wading in the waters that are up to the thigh won't understand the pressure that you have endured; they can't fathom the crush depth. You stay submerged because you know that you have experienced the deep and mysterious things of God, and surfacing is simply not an option, at least not until the mission is complete.

God is the only one who knows how long your mission will last. It could be hours, days, months, or even years. When you are living a life of submission, time becomes irrelevant. You are no longer consumed with the wanting of this flesh, rather, you are consumed with the mission. Remember, the mission is freedom! The mission is not war, it is the prevention of war. The mission is protecting the lives of the innocent. To be more specific to your spiritual walk, the mission is to seek and save the lost. Not that you, in your flesh can save anyone, but the Commander in Chief (Jesus) is the Savior.

Your mission is your life, but your life is not your own. Your mission is to accomplish the will of the Commander in Chief. Your mission is being

SUB-MISSION: The Silent Service

lived out every day while never being accomplished until the mission is over: until your life is over. For those of you who choose to live a life of submission, you must understand that there are no days off. You cannot vacation apart from your mission. Surfacing cannot be optional to you, and if it is, then you will fall prey to your own carnality, losing the battle, and ultimately losing the war.

You were designed to dive! You were created to conquer. Do not think for a moment that surfacing will ease your pain and suffering; it will only make things worse. There are two types of surfacing that I want to talk about. The first is surfacing in your flesh, or in your pride. When you surface, or attempt to rise to the top in your own pride and arrogance, it should be no surprise what will be the result. The Scripture tells us of one who attempted to surface in his own pride and arrogance, and it was a complete disaster.

Satan, in the beginning, was the most beautiful angel in Heaven. He was responsible for directing all worship, in music and singing, toward God. It's possible that he had done his job well for many millennia. However, while attempting to surface, or exalt himself above the throne of God, he was ultimately cast down into the earth, which is God's footstool.

Son of man, say unto the prince of Tyrus, Thus saith the Lord GOD; Because thine heart is lifted up, and thou hast said, I am a God, I sit in the seat of God, in the midst of the seas; yet thou art a man, and not God, though thou set thine heart as the heart of God:

Ezekiel 28:2 KJV

Therefore thus saith the Lord G<small>OD</small>; Because thou hast set thine heart as the heart of God; Behold, therefore I will bring strangers upon thee, the terrible of the nations: and they shall draw their swords against the beauty of thy wisdom, and they shall defile thy brightness. They shall bring thee down to the pit, and thou shalt die the deaths of them that are slain in the midst of the seas.

Ezekiel 28:6-8 KJV

Thine heart was lifted up because of thy beauty, thou hast corrupted thy wisdom by reason of thy brightness: I will cast thee to the ground, I will lay thee before kings, that they may behold thee.

Ezekiel 28:17 KJV

SUB-MISSION: The Silent Service

Notice the reason why Satan's heart was lifted up; it was because of his beauty. In other words, Satan was more focused on his own image than on the image of God. He was captivated by his own beauty, insomuch that he took that and used it as a reason to surface or elevate, to be equal with God. He surfaced in his own pride and self-indulgence and thus was cast out of Heaven, down into the earth, and his ultimate demise will be eternity spent in the lake of fire. This is what self-promotion, pride, and ego in oneself looks like. Make no mistake, God will not put up with this type of behavior and allow you to remain in His presence.

Satan, or sometimes known as Lucifer (light-bearer), had participated in glorifying God, singing praises to His name alongside all the other angels, for ages. These angels would have been illuminated by the light of God's glorious presence, and it was their job to reflect that glory back to its source and creator, God. However, and for whatever reason, Lucifer decided rather than to reflect this glory back to God, he would absorb it for himself. I believe that is how he came to even realize his own beauty; he used God's glorious light to reveal something about himself that did not need to even be realized.

This is exactly what happens to people today; they start out good, living for God and glorifying Him until they misuse the goodness of God to illuminate their God given gifting, and rather than giving credit to God and remaining humble, they misplace the credit, creating a breeding ground for pride to grow. If you do realize that God has gifted you in some way, you better turn back to God and say, its only due to the goodness of God that I have this gift. Else, your flesh will cause you to surface. However, God will not be equal with anyone, nor will He share His glory with another.

The second type of surfacing that I want to discuss is in the spirit, when our mission is complete and we are called to surface, not in pride but in humble submission. This event is known by several names, but I will use the following: rapture. There will be a day when the Lord will come back in like manner as He left, descending from the clouds, and in that moment, the dead in Christ will rise to meet the Lord in the air. Then, those of us who are alive and remain on the earth will be caught up (raptured) to meet them in the air.

> *For the Lord himself shall descend from heaven with a shout, with the voice of the archangel, and with the trump of God: and the dead in Christ shall rise first: Then we which are alive and remain shall be caught up together with them in the clouds, to meet the Lord in the air: and so shall we ever be with the Lord.*
>
> *1 Thessalonians 4:16-17 KJV*

SUB-MISSION: The Silent Service

Until this great and terrible day of the Lord comes, we would do well to reside within the crush depth zone. Living a life of submission is the only way that we can safeguard ourselves against pride creeping in and destroying us. A sailor once said, "Remember, we are the silent service, and we serve with silent pride." When we understand this, we will be more apt to do more listening and less talking as submission is silent and pride is loud. Again, when you are living a life of submission, you don't require to be heard, at least not by those in this world. You can make your complaints and petitions known to God who is able to bring justice and peace unlike no other.

When you surface to meet the Lord in the air, the opportunity will have passed to make excuses as to why you have not dealt with pride in your life. There is no better time than the present to choose to dive. Dive into a life of submission. Submit to God and let Him lead and guide your life. Submit to His voice and listen intently as He directs your every move. Submit to your pastor as your shepherd and trust His relationship with God enough to freely speak into and over your life, providing not only sound doctrine, but wisdom in the Holy Ghost. Submit to the leadership of the church (godly men and women) and allow some to sit at your table and offer godly council as you walk with God.

Submit to change when directed by the Spirit of God that change is needed. Submit to correction when it's given in love, regardless of who it comes from. Submit yourselves one to another and never be too proud to admit that you were wrong. Godly submission will teach you to apologize even if you know that you were in the right. A godly man or woman will seek restoration rather than retaliation. Submission is not self-serving. Rather, it is quite the opposite; submission is positioning yourself to serve others.

If you seek to surface based on anything outside of the completion of the mission, you can be sure that pride is at the helm and you are not in control; better said, God is not in control. And when God is not in control, chaos is sure to ensue.

I've heard it said, the only thing stronger than the will of God is the will of man. It's not that God can't stop us, it's that He won't stop us. God will allow you to surface if you so desire, but that's just it, it's your desire. The Scripture says, *"Delight thyself also in the LORD; And he shall give thee the desires of thine heart"*

I believe that the Lord will give you the desire of your heart, no matter what it is. If you choose to ignore the call of the master to turn from your wicked ways, repent of your sins, be baptized in His name, and receive the gift of the Holy Ghost, then He will give you over to your desires, a life void of His presence. But if you choose to run to an altar, ask God to forgive you and let Him clean you up through the waters of baptism in His name, and receive His Spirit, He will give you your desires, and you can make your calling and election sure, having your name written down in the Lamb's book of life.

One final time, let us look back on our life aboard our submarine and remember the feeling we felt when we received the word from the XO, "Ladies and gentlemen, it's time to head home." Oh, the joy that filled that boat as our long journey of silence was coming to an end. Each one of us had spent months, and some years, living a life of complete silence aboard that submarine. We sacrificed our conveniences for the sake of the greater good: the people. While this journey was hard and no doubt, sometimes we wanted to surface, we refused to quit and stayed the course until we heard those faithful words, "It's time to head home."

As the submarine broke through the surface of the water, and the hatch of the conning tower was opened, our eyes were pierced with sunlight that we hadn't seen in a long time. The smell of fresh air, and the sound of songbirds singing the Lord's praise filled the boat as we steered the boat into its final resting place: the harbor. With friends and family anxiously awaiting our arrival, this day would come to be the greatest reunion of our lives.

Stepping off the boat, onto the solid ground beneath, we were overcome with emotion, and our hearts were filled with joy! We were finally home. All the training and hard work had paid off, and we could finally rest, knowing that we had nearly completed our mission. However, there was one final step that every submariner must take before being reunited with their loved ones. The mission was not fully over until we walked down the ramp from the boat to the pier, taking a moment to stand before the Commander in Chief for the final approval of a completed mission and a job well done.

Dressed in our "chokers" (Service Dress White), we stopped before the Commander in Chief, standing at attention and watched as he raised his right hand in salute as he uttered those faithful words, "Well done, you were faithful to the mission."

At the end of the day, surrounded by friends and family, knowing that I had completed the mission and had not surfaced too soon, I could honestly say, it was worth it all. All the blood, sweat, and tears that we poured into a life of submission aboard that boat were worth it all now that we were home. Sure, it was hard work and there was some pain along the way, but the pain was just a memory now. When

SUB-MISSION: The Silent Service

I got home, I could hardly remember the many sleepless nights where we were too afraid to close our eyes in fear of what may be lurking just outside of our vessel. I could finally rest, knowing that there is no longer a reason to fear.

CONCLUSION

Friend, allow me to speak into your life right now as I conclude this book. Submission is not an easy road to travel down, that you can be sure of. Submission is not the most popular trend out there. Submission is very hard work and is not seasonal. Submission is hard to start and even harder to finish. Submission is not for the weak or the temporary. Submission will try all your nerves, push all your buttons, test your patience, as well as your Holy Ghost. But there is one thing that is certain, submission works!

If you desire to leave the shallow waters of mediocrity and go deeper into the great things that God has planned for your life, you must learn submission. You must learn to shut down the untamed, unsubmitted thoughts that enter your mind. You must cast down every imagination of your flesh, submitting every thought to the power of the Holy Ghost and take on the mind of Christ to defeat your pride.

Just because you have repented, been baptized in Jesus' name, and have been filled with the Holy Ghost, doesn't make you exempt from the battle against pride. After all, Lucifer was literally in the very presence of God, but still, pride found a way inside of him. To learn submission, you must actively pursue it daily. To keep pride at bay, stay in alignment with the will of God, the vision of your pastor, and protect your own soul, you must learn submission.

If you are anything like me, you will likely fail at first. I can't tell you how many times that I tried to submit, just to find myself complaining about the very thing I was trying to place in God's hands. I failed time and time again, but there is something very powerful about a made-up mind. I was determined to get past my own arrogance, lay my anger and bitterness down at the feet of Jesus, and repent. I prayed, "God, forgive me and help me learn to submit. Help me not to be angry and bitter about this situation that is out of my control. Teach me to respond the way that you would respond. Help me learn submission."

Little by little, I have learned to become a bit more like Jesus and less like this world. I consumed as much godly instruction as I could find to help me get rid of pride in my life. You, too, can do the same. Read books, watch videos, write your feelings down, seek godly counsel from your pastor or someone else you trust. Talk to God about it. Do whatever you have to do to stay down. Do not surface too soon. Do not recoil or react, but rather, respond. Respond with submission, and if you do, one day you will hear those precious words, "Well done my good and faithful servant. You have been faithful over a few things, behold, I will make you a ruler over many."

I want to pray over you right now:

SUB-MISSION: The Silent Service

Jesus, thank you for allowing this person to read this book. Thank you for an opportunity to learn how to live a life of submission. Thank you for the desire that you have placed inside of them to be better: to be more like you. Thank you for the wisdom of your Word that leads and guides us. Thank you for the strength that they are receiving today through your Spirit. Thank you for never giving up on them. I pray that you will equip the reader of this book right now. I ask that you give them a desire to go deeper into their relationship with you.

I take authority and dominion over every spirit of pride right now, in the name of Jesus! I bind the spiritual wickedness that is in high places. I bind every principality, every power, and every ruler of the darkness of this world, in Jesus' name! By the power of Jesus' name, every stronghold will be broken, and every yoke of the enemy will be destroyed! God, remove any trace of self-righteousness, arrogance, or pride. Help me right now to learn submission. We are overcomers by the blood of the Lamb and by the word of our testimony. Amen.